© 2025 Michael Patrick.

Joy & Happiness: Returning to Loving Awareness

All rights reserved.

No part of this publication may be reproduced, stored in a retrieval system, or transmitted in any form or by any means-electronic, mechanical, photocopying, recording, or otherwise-without the prior written permission of the author, except in the case of brief quotations embodied in critical articles or reviews.

Cover art by Michael Patrick

Disclaimer

This book is not intended to be a substitute for professional mental health treatment, diagnosis, or therapy. It is a work of inspiration and reflection, designed to support personal insight and emotional healing.

If you are experiencing a mental health crisis, please seek immediate help from a licensed therapist, counselor, or medical professional. You are not alone, and support is available.

Your well-being matters.

Joy & Happiness:

Returning to Loving Awareness

Michael Patrick

2025

Preface

This is the book I wish someone else had written and given to me as a child.

Why are so many of us unhappy? Why do we suffer, feel disconnected, or live in patterns of fear, stress, and judgment?

This book offers a different kind of answer—not from the mind, but from the heart. We were all born as pure Loving Awareness: soft, open, radiant. But as we grew, we were conditioned. Traumas—both personal and generational—planted seeds of fear, shame, guilt, and self-doubt deep within us.

Slowly, a dense contraction formed in our body-mind system. These invisible distortions clouded our true nature. We learned to hide, to strive, to doubt our worth. We forgot who we really are.

Imagine that today is your first day on earth. You are looking at everything for the first time with awe and wonder. You are a manifestation of pure Loving Awareness. You are a divine gift from God, the creation, the Love-Beauty of existence itself.

And your brothers and sisters who are already here on Earth witness your pure Loving Awareness as a reminder of who they truly are—but many have long forgotten. I'm writing this book to remind the beautiful adults of the way back to our essence of pure Loving Awareness.

The root cause of suffering is not merely external. It's the forgetting of who we are. When we identify with fear, comparison, control, or ego, we separate from the joy that is always available in the present moment. But by tuning our attention to high-vibrational states—gratitude, compassion, presence, forgiveness, truth, simplicity, and joy—we begin to return. Not to some idealized version of ourselves, but to our original, undistorted essence.

Joy & Happiness: Returning to Loving Awareness
It is a book of 365 contemplations that gently guide you back to this essence.

Each reflection is a reminder to shift your attention—to witness, to feel, to breathe, to come home. Not through force, but through soft awareness.

This book is an offering of presence and possibility—a quiet companion to help you remember what the world may have caused you to forget.

The more we remember, the more we radiate. And the more we radiate, the more others remember, too.

Let this book be a daily anchor, A soft mirror, A whisper from the truth of who you are.

You are Loving Awareness. And that is enough.

The Invitation

You are not a victim of your state—you are its conductor. Your attention is a sacred tool. When you learn to gently and consistently redirect it toward light, you begin to live in alignment with your true nature: joy, presence, and love.

Here is a list of high vibrational states or frequencies of consciousness you can tune your attention to, like a spiritual radio dial:

Core High Vibrations to Tune Into
1. Loving Awareness – unconditional presence, the essence of divinity within all
2. Joy – pure delight in being, beyond cause
3. Gratitude – thankful reverence for existence
4. Peace – inner stillness, ease, and spacious calm
5. Wonder – childlike awe at the mystery of life
6. Compassion – feeling with others from the heart
7. Truth – deep alignment with what *is*, beyond illusion

8. Beauty – perceiving the sacred harmony in all things
9. Playfulness – lightness of spirit, spontaneous joy
10. Forgiveness – liberation from holding pain
11. Freedom – the felt sense of limitless being
12. Presence – full aliveness in the now
13. Innocence – original purity, unburdened seeing
14. Creativity – channeling the new through pure being
15. Trust – surrendering to the greater intelligence of life
16. Reverence – honoring all as sacred
17. Oneness – nonseparation from the Whole
18. Bliss – ecstatic unity with the Source
19. Stillness – vibrating silence, the womb of awareness
20. Abundance – recognizing the infinite giving of life

How do we align with our Loving-Awareness?

You can tune your attention to these by asking:

• *What does love feel like in this moment?*

• *Can I rest as peace right now, without needing a reason?*

• *What am I grateful for that I usually overlook?*

• *What beauty is quietly revealing itself to me right now?*

Attune the Heart: A Daily Vibrational Compass

Breathe into Love
Let your awareness settle in the quiet warmth that holds all things gently.

Drink the Light of Joy
Not because of a reason, but because joy is your birthright frequency.

Whisper Thank You
Feel the hush of gratitude, even for the unseen blessings.

Sink into Peace
Let your nervous system exhale. Let silence cradle your being.

Wonder Like a Child
Gaze again with eyes unburdened by conclusions.

Hold Compassion Lightly

Cradle others in the kindness you long to receive.

Speak Only What Rings True

Let your words hum with the vibration of honesty.

Notice Beauty in the Ordinary

A shadow on the wall. The way light moves. A leaf.

Play with Existence

Make it a game. Make it art. Make it a dance.

Release Through Forgiveness

Drop the heavy bags. They were never your true inheritance.

Stretch into Freedom

You are not the cage. You are the breeze that slips through.

Come Home to Presence

Everything you seek is blooming in this moment.

Remember Innocence
Before the story, before the scar—there was just open sky.

Create from the Deep Stream
Let inspiration rise from the eternal spring within.

Trust the Mystery
It's okay not to know. The unknown is not an enemy.

Bow in Reverence
Every breath, a miracle. Every soul, a spark of the Infinite.

Feel the Oneness
No edges. No other. Just the one Light playing as many.

Rest in Bliss
Let yourself be absorbed in the sweetness of Being.

Melt into Stillness

Not absence, but fullness without motion.

Receive Abundance

Not in possessions, but in the overflowing richness of each sacred moment.

Day 1

Return to Loving Awareness

You are not the wound.

You are the one who sees it with love.

Return again to the space behind the ache.

Day 2

Joy Without Cause

Joy doesn't wait for reasons.

It dances barefoot in the unknown.

Let it rise without permission.

Day 3

Gratitude in the Smallest Places

Thank the quiet spoon. The warm cup. The breath.

Gratitude hides in humble corners.

Go looking.

Day 4

The Silence That Sings

In the stillness beyond noise,

there is a song with no sound.

Be still enough to hear it.

Day 5

The Sky Within

Inside you is a sky with no ceiling.

Let your thoughts be passing clouds.

You are the space that holds them.

Day 6

Freedom Is Not Far

It's not in the next step—

it's in this one,

when you stop trying to be someone else.

Day 7

Let Beauty Find You

Beauty doesn't demand attention—

it waits, shyly,

for the one who slows down.

Day 8

Compassion Begins with You

Before you soften toward others,

offer your own pain a gentle hand.

You are worthy of mercy.

Day 9

Playfulness Is Sacred

Laughing is a form of worship.

Play is a portal.

Even God giggles sometimes.

Day 10

You Are Already Whole

There is no piece missing.

You only forgot the shape of your light.

Wholeness has never left you.

Day 11

Trust the Mystery

You don't have to know to be held.

The unknown is a womb, not a threat.

Let go and float.

Day 12

The Light Behind the Storm

Even in breakdown, light waits.

The storm cannot erase the sun.

Trust what is hidden to reappear.

Day 13

Peace Is Not Earned

You don't have to achieve calm.

It's already within you,

beneath the waves.

Day 14

Let It Be Enough

This moment is a whole universe.

Don't shrink it with "not enough."

Let what is be full.

Day 15

You Belong to the Divine

You are not lost—you are a spark of the Divine

remembering.

Even your doubts shimmer with divine Love.

Day 16

Forgiveness Is Freedom

Not forgetting. Not condoning.

Just releasing the chain that binds *you*.

Be the one who drops the rope.

Day 17

The Sacred Ordinary

The miracle is not far away.

It is tea. Skin. Dust motes in light.

See what's always been holy.

Day 18

No Need to Hurry

Time is not chasing you.

You are carried, not rushed.

Let presence set the pace.

Day 19

Oneness Lives in Your Breath

There is no separation
when you feel the inhale of a tree.
We all breathe each other.

Day 20

Let the Heart Lead

Logic may map the terrain,
but only the heart can walk it.
Let love show you the way.

Day 21

The Power of Softness

You don't need to be hard to be strong.
Softness holds mountains.
Let gentleness be your armor.

Day 22

Presence Is the Portal

You've been waiting at the gate of the future.

But the miracle was always

here.

Day 23

The Invitation of Wonder

You don't have to understand.

You only need to marvel.

Wonder will do the rest.

Day 24

You Are Not Behind

There is no race.

Your timing is sacred,

even when it looks slow.

Day 25

Awaken the Eyes of the Soul

The soul doesn't look with judgment.

It sees beauty in the bruises.

Try seeing as it does.

Day 26

Sink into Enoughness

You don't need another reason to be.

You are already valid,

even in stillness.

Day 27

Let Go with Love

Release is not rejection.

Letting go is a love song to life.

Sing it gently.

Day 28

The Whole Universe Hums Within

You are not apart from it.

You *are* the humming,

the stardust, the silence, the flame.

Day 29

Abide in What Is

Stop grasping at "better."

Rest in what already is.

It is enough. So are you.

Day 30

The Sacred Pause of Awareness

Before reacting,

there is a breath.

That breath is where your freedom lives.

Day 31

Truth Feels Like Relief

When you find truth,

your shoulders drop.

The body recognizes what the mind forgets.

Day 32

Choose Resonance Over Rules

Not all paths are for your feet.

Walk only where your soul hums.

Let resonance be your guide.

Day 33

Love Needs No Justification

You don't have to explain

why your heart opens.

Just let it bloom.

Day 34

Celebrate Small Joys

Joy isn't always fireworks.

Sometimes it's the way

your favorite mug fits your hands.

Day 35

Stillness Is Alive

Stillness is not emptiness—

it is vibrant, pulsing being.

Go there often.

Day 36

Let Awe Find You

Stand under the sky.

Be as small as you can be.

That's where awe enters.

Day 37

There Is Nothing to Fix

You are not a project.

You are a garden.

Water, and witness the bloom.

Day 38

The Heart Doesn't Rush

It beats in its own rhythm,

always here.

Let it lead.

Day 39

You Are a Living Poem

No need to rhyme.

Just breathe and exist.

You are already beautiful.

Day 40

The Light Is Always Underneath

Darkness isn't your enemy—

it's the invitation to remember

the light you carry.

Day 41

Becoming Is Beautiful

You don't need to be finished to be radiant.

Even the becoming shines.

Day 42

Let Simplicity Speak

Complexity can confuse the heart.

Simplicity speaks in whispers—

clear, kind, and true.

Day 43

Honor Your Sensitivity

Sensitivity isn't weakness—

it's refined perception.

You feel what others miss.

Day 44

Every Breath Is Sacred

Breathe as if kissed by God.

Because you are.

Right now. Always.

Day 45

Be Lighthearted with Life

Not everything needs to be heavy.

Let life laugh through you

sometimes.

Day 46

Love the Process

The path *is* the masterpiece.

Even the missteps leave sacred footprints.

Day 47

Your Essence Is Untouched

No experience has stained your core.

Your essence is light,

unbreakable and pure.

Day 48

Silence Holds You

When words fall away,

a deeper presence wraps around you.

It needs no sound to say: *I am here.*

Day 49

Bask in Enough

Enough is not mediocre—

it's majestic.

Practice basking in what *is*.

Day 50

Your Light Was Never Lost

Only forgotten.

Covered.

Dimmed by stories that were never yours.

Day 51

Let Life Surprise You

You don't need to predict it all.

Let the unknown show you

its quiet miracles.

Day 52

Rest Is Holy

You are not lazy.

You are a soul

that needs soft ground to bloom.

Day 53

Release Comparison

You are not here to be someone else.

Comparison dims the light

you were born to shine.

Day 54

Receive Without Guilt

You don't have to earn what is freely given.

Let love pour in

and simply say thank you.

Day 55

Live as a Blessing

You don't need a grand gesture.

A glance, a kind word,

a silent prayer—they all bless.

Day 56

Trust Your Inner Compass

Your intuition knows the way.

It's older than logic

and truer than fear.

Day 57

Let Nature Heal You

Sit beneath a tree.

Let the sky clear your thoughts.

The Earth remembers who you are.

Day 58

You're Allowed to Feel It All

Don't numb the ache.

Even sorrow belongs.

Let your humanity be sacred.

Day 59

Radiate Without Shrinking

Don't dim to make others comfortable.

Shine with softness—

not apology.

Day 60

God Is in the Glimpse

Not always a thunderclap—

sometimes just

a breeze on your cheek, reminding you.

Day 61

Love Is Who You Are

It's not something you give.

It's something you *are*

when you stop pretending otherwise.

Day 62

You Are Held

Even when it feels like falling,

you are being carried

by something timeless.

Day 63

Celebrate the Small Wins

Not every victory roars.

Some whisper—

you showed up, and that was enough.

Day 64

Let Presence Be the Goal

Forget achievement for a moment.

Presence is a destination

you're always already in.

Day 65

Speak Light into the Day

Your words cast spells.

Use them to build bridges,

not walls.

Day 66

Nothing Needs to Be Perfect

Let the imperfect shine.

Let the mess breathe.

Life is more art than answer.

Day 67

The Heart Knows What the Mind Can't

Don't wait for logic to catch up.

Let the heart's whisper guide your steps.

Day 68

Rest Inside the Moment

No effort. No reaching.

Just let the now

wrap around you.

Day 69

The Path Is Always Beneath You

You haven't lost your way.

You're on it—

even when you can't see the road.

Day 70

Let Yourself Be Surprised by Peace

Sometimes, peace arrives unannounced—

in the middle of chaos.

Welcome it in.

Day 71

Your Light Is Contagious

When you shine,

others remember their glow.

Radiate anyway.

Day 72

Listen Beyond the Noise

There's a deeper voice beneath the static.

It speaks in stillness

and knows your name.

Day 73

Flow with What Arises

Resistance tightens the soul.

Flow loosens it

into grace.

Day 74

Stay Open to Wonder

Cynicism ages the spirit.

Wonder keeps you young

and wide-eyed with divinity.

Day 75

Live Gently

Your power is in your softness.

Move like water—

persistent, nourishing, calm.

Day 76

Be Your Own Sanctuary

Create quiet within.

Let your own heart

be a temple of return.

Day 77

The Now Is Sacred Ground

Stop searching for holy places.

This moment,

exactly as it is, is the altar.

Day 78

You Are Allowed to Begin Again

Every breath is a restart.

There is no shame

in starting over.

Day 79

Let Light Enter the Cracks

You don't have to be whole

to be radiant.

Your cracks are doorways for grace.

Day 80

Celebrate That You're Here

You made it to this moment.

That alone

is a quiet kind of miracle.

Day 81

Peace Doesn't Need a Reason

Let peace arrive without explanation.

No fixing. No forcing.

Just soft, effortless being.

Day 82

Be Gentle with the Process

Healing takes time and tenderness.

Rush nothing.

Love every step.

Day 83

Let Awe Be Your Compass

Go where your soul gasps in wonder.

That's the path.

Follow it.

Day 84

There Is Wisdom in the Pause

When nothing moves,

the soul listens deeper.

Don't fear the stillness.

Day 85

Let Yourself Be Seen

You are not too much.

You are not too little.

You are *real,* and that is enough.

Day 86

You're Growing Even When It's Hard to See

Growth isn't always loud.

Sometimes, it's underground—

quiet and sacred.

Day 87

Choose Light Thoughts

Your thoughts plant the garden.

Choose the ones that bloom joy

and kindness.

Day 88

Come Back to the Body

Your body is not a burden—

it's your home.

Breathe it back into belonging.

Day 89

Sacredness Is in the Ordinary

Don't wait for miracles.

The divine wears the disguise

of daily life.

Day 90

Be the Calm You Crave

Don't seek it outside—

become it.

Let your presence ripple out.

Day 91

Let Go of What's Not Yours

Not every feeling is your own.
Return what never belonged
with Love.

Day 92

Open to Inner Guidance

There's a quiet knowing inside.
It doesn't yell—
but it never lies.

Day 93

Don't Forget the Sky

When life feels heavy,
look up.
The sky still believes in you.

Day 94

You Are Allowed to Change

You don't owe anyone the old you.

Grow in new directions.

It's sacred evolution.

Day 95

Celebrate Your Sensitivity

You notice beauty others miss.

Feel deeply.

It's your gift, not your flaw.

Day 96

There Is Strength in Surrender

Surrender isn't giving up.

It's opening up.

Let grace carry you.

Day 97

Live in Alignment, Not Approval

Let your soul guide you—

not the need to be liked.

Truth is more nourishing than praise.

Day 98

Let the Moment Hold You

Fall into the arms of now.

It has room for everything—

including you.

Day 99

Softness Is Revolutionary

In a hard world,

your softness heals.

Keep choosing it.

Day 100

Celebrate Your Aliveness

You are breath and heartbeat,

stardust and spirit.

You are here—and that's everything.

Day 101

Let Light Guide the Way

When you don't know what to do,

follow what feels warm,

kind, and quietly true.

Day 102

Rest in the Unknown

You don't need to force clarity.

The unknown holds you

until it's time to know.

Day 103

Let Beauty Interrupt You

Stop mid-thought for the flower.

Pause for the light in someone's eyes.

Beauty is trying to get your attention.

Day 104

You Are a Sacred Flame

You weren't meant to stay hidden.

Shine softly,

but shine fully.

Day 105

Every Ending Has a Gift

What leaves carves space

for what longs to enter.

Grieve, but stay open.

Day 106

Breathe into What Hurts

Don't run from pain.

Let the breath hold it

until it softens into wisdom.

Day 107

Stay Close to Your Soul

Don't trade your essence

for approval, applause, or ease.

Your soul knows the way home.

Day 108

The Present Moment Is Medicine

When your thoughts race,

drop into the now.

Let presence soothe the ache.

Day 109

Let Joy Be Unconditional

Joy is not a reward.

It's your essence,

waiting to be remembered.

Day 110

Trust the Inner Bloom

You don't need to rush your unfolding.

You are a flower

with divine timing.

Day 111

Let Silence Be Your Teacher

In silence,

you meet the parts of you

that truth still whispers to.

Day 112

Embrace the Mystery

Not everything needs to be solved.

Some things need only

to be honored.

Day 113

You Are a Thread of the Divine

Not separate,

but seamlessly woven

into the fabric of God.

Day 114

You Don't Have to Have It All Together

You're allowed to be undone.

Let love hold the pieces

without rushing to fix them.

Day 115

Even the Dark Has Wisdom

The dark is not your enemy.

It is the space

where roots are born.

Day 116

Simplicity Heals the Spirit

What if less

could be more holy?

Strip away, and see.

Day 117

Bless What You've Been Through

Every scar carries a chapter.

You survived.

That deserves blessing.

Day 118

You Are Worthy Right Now

Not when you achieve.

Not when you're healed.

Right now. Just as you are.

Day 119

Let Love Be Enough

Love doesn't have to be loud.

Sometimes, it's just staying.

Sometimes, it's a quiet yes.

Day 120

Anchor in Grace

Grace holds you

even when you forget it's there.

Let it be your foundation.

Day 121

Let Your Breath Be Your Anchor

When the world spins fast,

return to breath.

It knows the way to center.

Day 122

You Are the Witness

You are not the storm.

You are the one

watching it pass.

Day 123

Dare to Feel Deeply

You weren't meant for numbness.

Your depth is your gift—

feel all the way through.

Day 124

Let This Moment Be Enough

You don't need to chase the extraordinary.

The quiet now

holds more than you think.

Day 125

Shine Quietly

Not all light blinds.

Some glows soft,

and warms the whole room.

Day 126

Let Life Be Art

Every breath a brushstroke,

every word a color—

paint your day with care.

Day 127

Be Gentle as You Grow

Growth is not linear.

Some days stretch.

Some simply soften.

Day 128

You Are Not Broken

You've bent, you've burned, you've bled—

but you are still

whole in your essence.

Day 129

Miracles Come in Quiet Ways

A shift in perspective.

A tear that heals.

A breeze at just the right time.

Day 130

Release What You've Outgrown

Not everything meant to begin

is meant to stay.

Make room.

Day 131

Let Love Flow Without Agenda

Don't try to earn it.

Don't try to control it.

Just let it move through you.

Day 132

You Are a Living Expression of Grace

Not something to strive for—

something you already are,

by simply being.

Day 133

Speak to Yourself with Kindness

Be the voice you longed to hear.

Gentleness changes everything.

Day 134

Flow, Don't Force

What's meant for you

won't need to be pushed.

Just opened to.

Day 135

Light Doesn't Apologize

It just shines.

So should you.

Day 136

Let the Earth Remind You

Roots grow slow.

Trees sway.

Everything softens in time.

Day 137

Celebrate How Far You've Come

Even if you're not "there,"

you're not where you were.

Honor the road behind you.

Day 138

You Don't Need to Prove Anything

You're not here to earn your worth.

You *are* it.

Simply by existing.

Day 139

Let Each Day Be a Blessing

Not because it's perfect—

but because you showed up

with an open heart.

Day 140

You Are the Light You're Looking For

Not out there—

in here.

Shining quietly, always.

Day 141

Breathe Before You Speak

Let stillness touch your words.

The breath brings clarity

before sound becomes shape.

Day 142

The Present Is Always Enough

You don't need to reach forward.

Let now

unfold its quiet gift.

Day 143

Let Softness Lead

A soft gaze,

a gentle word—

sometimes these shift the world more than force.

Day 144

Healing Happens in Layers

You won't fix it all in a day.

But every breath

is a gentle return.

Day 145

You Are Not Your Thoughts

Let them come and go like birds.

You are the open sky

they fly through.

Day 146

Let Go of What Closes You

Not everything deserves space in your heart.

Choose what expands.

Release what contracts.

Day 147

Honor Your Quiet Victories

Some triumphs come

without applause—

a breath held, a boundary kept, a tear released.

Day 148

Let Ease Be a Guide

If it flows with grace,

you may be walking the path

meant just for you.

Day 149

You Don't Need to Explain Your Peace

Let others misunderstand if they must.

You've found your stillness—

keep it sacred.

Day 150

Listen with Your Whole Being

Not to respond,

but to receive.

Deep listening is a form of love.

Day 151

Your Essence Is Unchanging

No matter what life adds or takes,

your core remains—

pure and untouched.

Day 152

Let Beauty Be a Language

It speaks in sunlight,

in laughter,

in the curve of leaves.

Day 153

Stillness Is Strength

Not frozen,

but rooted.

Be the mountain beneath the wind.

Day 154

Joy Can Be Quiet

It doesn't always dance.
Sometimes it sits with you
in silence, smiling.

Day 155

Let Grace Rewrite the Story

You are not the worst thing that's happened.
Let grace hold the pen now.

Day 156

Be Present to Your Own Life

Don't miss the miracle
by scrolling through someone else's.

Day 157

Let Curiosity Lead You Back to Wonder

Ask with your heart.

Seek without fear.

Wonder is the birthplace of awe.

Day 158

You Deserve Peace Without Earning It

No need to strive.

You're already worthy

of peace, rest, and tenderness.

Day 159

Speak Only What Lifts

Let your words be seeds

that grow flowers in someone else's day.

Day 160

You Are Already Aligned

Even when it feels off,

something deeper is holding you steady.

Trust it.

Day 161

Let Silence Restore You

When the noise gets loud,

return to the quiet within—

it never left you.

Day 162

You Don't Have to Carry It All

Set something down today.

Let the weight of the world

rest where it no longer belongs.

Day 163

Open Gently

Your heart is not a gate to be forced.

It opens like a flower,

when the light is right.

Day 164

Let Presence Be Enough

No need to perform or prove.

Your being here

is already everything.

Day 165

The Soul Moves at Its Own Pace

Honor the rhythm

that cannot be rushed.

Trust the slow unfolding.

Day 166

Let Wonder Wash Over You

Stand in the rain.

Stare at the moon.

Let the world astonish you again.

Day 167

Compassion Starts Within

You can't pour from an empty heart.

Offer yourself

the love you offer others.

Day 168

You Are Allowed to Not Know

Certainty is not required.

Only honesty,

and a willingness to see.

Day 169

Let Beauty Catch You Off Guard

Stop mid-thought

for the way the light hits a leaf.

Beauty heals in flashes.

Day 170

Your Worth Is Not in Productivity

You are not your output.

You are a living miracle,

even on your quietest days.

Day 171

Trust the Invisible Work

Even when nothing shows,

something within

is growing roots.

Day 172

You Are Safe to Be Soft

The world needs less armor,

more tenderness.

Let yourself be soft.

Day 173

Receive the Day Like a Gift

You didn't have to wake up—

but you did.

Let that be enough for awe.

Day 174

Let Your Energy Speak for You

Sometimes the most powerful presence

is simply peace

entering a room.

Day 175

Let Go with Kindness

Not every goodbye must be bitter.

Some endings

are blessings in disguise.

Day 176

The Universe Moves Through You

You're not separate from it.

You are the current

and the wave.

Day 177

Celebrate Small Moments of Clarity

Even a glimpse

is a holy thing.

Let it land.

Day 178

The Now Is Enough to Begin Again

You don't need a new year,

a full plan,

or anyone's permission.

Day 179

Let Peace Be Your Compass

If it costs your peace,

it's not the path.

Let ease light the way.

Day 180

You Are the Calm in the Chaos

The storm is outside—

but the eye of the storm

is you.

Day 181

You Are Not Alone in This Moment

Even when you feel isolated,

something unseen holds you—

a quiet presence, always near.

Day 182

Let Your Breath Be Your Refuge

Each inhale is a return.

Each exhale, a release.

You are never far from peace.

Day 183

You Can Begin Again at Any Time

A single moment of awareness

can turn the tide.

Start from here.

Day 184

Let Your Heart Stay Open

Even after hurt,

let love rise again.

This is how we heal the world.

Day 185

Your Energy Is Sacred

Not everything deserves access.

Protect what glows within you.

Day 186

Gentleness Is a Superpower

In a loud world,

gentleness is revolutionary.

Lead with softness.

Day 187

Let the Small Things Matter

A kind glance,

a warm tea,

a deep sigh—they add up to everything.

Day 188

Be the Peace You Seek

You are the source.

Let peace ripple from within.

Day 189

You Were Never Meant to Be Perfect

Perfection is a myth.

Your humanity is enough.

Day 190

Open to the Quiet Joys

There is joy in folding laundry,

watering plants,

watching clouds. Receive it.

Day 191

Let Your True Self Lead

Not the mask.

Not the role.

But the quiet truth beneath it all.

Day 192

Even the Pause Has Purpose

When nothing moves,

something deep is shifting.

Trust the stillness.

Day 193

You Are Allowed to Feel Good

Joy is not selfish.

It is sacred.

Let yourself have it.

Day 194

Be Fully Here, Just Once Today

Even for a moment—

feel the floor, taste the air,

come home to now.

Day 195

Let Beauty Break Your Heart Open

Sometimes it's too much—

a sky too wide,

a kindness too pure. Let it break you open.

Day 196

Don't Rush to Understand

Some things are meant

to be felt,

not figured out.

Day 197

You Can Be Both Healing and Whole

You are not unfinished.

You are a whole being

in the process of remembering.

Day 198

Rest When You're Weary

You don't have to earn it.

Rest is not a luxury—

it is a right.

Day 199

The Soul Recognizes What Is True

Even when the mind doubts,

your soul knows.

Let it speak.

Day 200

Celebrate the Light You Carry

You've walked through so much

and still you shine.

Let yourself be seen.

Day 201

Your Presence Is Enough

You don't have to say the perfect thing.

Just being here

can be the greatest gift.

Day 202

Let the Mind Rest

You're allowed to not analyze, fix, or solve.

Let your mind

simply rest in quiet awareness.

Day 203

Your Path Is Sacred

Even if it looks different.

Even if it winds and dips.

It's yours—and it's holy.

Day 204

Feel the Ground Beneath You

Let the earth remind you:

you are supported,

even when life feels uncertain.

Day 205

Let Go of the Need to Know

You don't have to predict every outcome.

Trust that clarity comes

in its own time.

Day 206

You Are Not Too Much

Your emotions, your depth, your voice—

they're not excess.

They're soul.

Day 207

Be Gentle with Unfinished Things

Let the unanswered questions live.

Let the mess be okay.

Let patience be your peace.

Day 208

Trust the Wisdom of Your Body

Your body speaks.

Not in words,

but in feeling, tension, ease—listen.

Day 209

You Are More Than What You Do

You are not your job.

Not your task list.

You are a being, not a machine.

Day 210

Soothe Yourself with Kindness

Speak to yourself the way you would

to someone you love.

Let your words be warm.

Day 211

Let Peace Be the Practice

Not the goal.

Not the reward.

But the way.

Day 212

Nothing About You Is a Mistake

The way you feel.

The way you love.

The way you see. All of it—on purpose.

Day 213

Return to Simplicity

Not everything needs to be fixed or figured out.

Let today be enough

just as it is.

Day 214

You Are Already on Time

Life isn't behind you.

You're not late.

You're aligned with your own unfolding.

Day 215

Soft Is Still Strong

You can be gentle

and still move mountains.

Kindness has power.

Day 216

Let the Day Unfold

Don't grip so tightly.

Let today surprise you.

Let life breathe.

Day 217

Release the Old Story

You're not bound

to the version of you

that didn't know what you know now.

Day 218

Let Stillness Show You the Way

Stillness doesn't stall you—

it aligns you

with what truly matters.

Day 219

Your Light Helps Others Remember Theirs

When you shine honestly,

you awaken what's asleep

in those around you.

Day 220

Let Love Be What Guides You

Not fear.

Not guilt.

Only love—gently leading the way.

Day 221

You Are a Beacon of Calm

When you choose stillness,

you help others find their breath.

Your calm is contagious.

Day 222

Let Go of Harsh Expectations

You are not here to be perfect.

You are here to be real,

and that is enough.

Day 223

Live in Alignment, Not Obligation

Choose what resonates.

Let go of the "shoulds."

Your joy is a compass.

Day 224

You Can Hold Contradictions

You can be strong and uncertain.

Grieving and grateful.

The soul is wide enough for both.

Day 225

Presence Is a Kind of Prayer

Being fully here—

with what is, as it is—

is sacred in itself.

Day 226

Let the Day Hold You

You don't have to control everything.

Let the light, the rhythm,

the moment carry you.

Day 227

Feel What Needs to Be Felt

You don't have to suppress or analyze.

Just feel it.

That's enough.

Day 228

Joy Can Be a Rebellion

In a weary world,

choosing joy is radical.

Let yourself smile without reason.

Day 229

Be the Safe Place You Seek

You are allowed to be your own sanctuary.

Speak gently.

Wrap yourself in compassion.

Day 230

Let What's True Be Simple

The deepest truths

are often the softest.

Listen for the quiet ones.

Day 231

You Belong Exactly as You Are

No changes required.

No roles to play.

You are already home.

Day 232

Follow the Subtle Pull

The soul doesn't shout.

It whispers.

Let its pull guide you inward.

Day 233

Rest Is a Sacred Yes

Saying yes to rest

is saying yes to life.

Honor your need for pause.

Day 234

Let Gratitude Change the View

You don't need a new life—

just a new lens.

Gratitude is that lens.

Day 235

It's Okay to Be Quiet Today

Let silence speak for you.

Stillness can say

what words cannot.

Day 236

Your Existence Is Enough

Even if you did nothing today—

you were still radiant

just by being.

Day 237

Listen for What Feels Alive

Not everything that calls

is meant for you.

Follow what makes you come alive.

Day 238

You're Allowed to Take Up Space

Expand without apology.

You are not too much.

You are perfectly placed.

Day 239

Trust the Gentle Unfolding

You don't bloom by force.

Trust the slow,

sweet rhythm of your own becoming.

Day 240

Let This Be a Healing Day

Let every breath

be a soft yes

to beginning again.

Day 241

Let Your Energy Speak First

Before the words,

your presence arrives.

Let it be warm, kind, and true.

Day 242

You Are the Pause Between Heartbeats

In the space between doing,

you exist fully.

Let the stillness define you, too.

Day 243

You're Allowed to Not Be Okay

Wholeness doesn't mean constant ease.

Let the hard days be held

with softness.

Day 244

Let Your Joy Be Unapologetic

Don't shrink to make others comfortable.

Your joy may remind them

of their own.

Day 245

There's Magic in Ordinary Moments

The mundane is a myth.

There's wonder

in folding towels and watching sunlight shift.

Day 246

Let What's Meant for You Find You

You don't have to chase.

What's aligned will arrive

with peace.

Day 247

You Are More Than One Moment

No single day defines you.

You are the collection of resilience,

hope, and return.

Day 248

Wholeness Includes Every Feeling

You are not "off"

when you're sad or still.

You are simply human.

Day 249

Rest Is a Way of Trusting

Trust that you don't need to strive

to be loved.

Pause, and receive.

Day 250

You're Already Worthy of Good Things

Not later,

not after healing.

Now.

Day 251

Let Nature Be Your Reminder

The trees aren't in a hurry.

The sky doesn't ask for applause.

They simply *are*.

Day 252

Be Willing to Be Changed by Peace

Let peace not only soothe you—

but rearrange you

into something softer.

Day 253

There Is No "Wrong" Way to Feel

Your feelings are bridges

to deeper truth.

Let them be.

Day 254

Surrender Can Be Sweet

Let go not with fear,

but with the trust

of a leaf on the breeze.

Day 255

Speak What's Real, Even Softly

You don't have to be loud

to be honest.

Truth doesn't need volume.

Day 256

You Are Here for a Reason

Not a task—

a presence,

a vibration only you carry.

Day 257

Breathe and Let It Pass

Storms don't last.

Emotions rise and fall.

Let the breath carry you through.

Day 258

Let Self-Compassion Be Your Practice

You don't need to be harsh

to be accountable.

Be gentle and grow.

Day 259

What You Feel Matters

Don't minimize your truth.

Your feelings are not too much—

they're messengers.

Day 260

Let This Moment Be a New Start

Begin again,

without punishment,

without pressure—just presence.

Day 261

You Are Already Becoming

Even when you feel still,

you are growing

in ways the world cannot see.

Day 262

Let Peace Arrive Uninvited

Don't wait for circumstances to settle.

Peace can enter

even in the middle of chaos.

Day 263

You Don't Need to Have the Answers

The questions themselves

are sacred.

Let them stay open.

Day 264

Let What's Real Be Enough

You don't need filters, fixes, or roles.

The real you

is radiant already.

Day 265

Offer Yourself the Benefit of the Doubt

You're doing the best you can

with what you know.

Be fair to yourself.

Day 266

Let Joy Break the Pattern

Even if it comes suddenly—

in laughter, in light—

let it break through.

Day 267

You Are Not Behind

The soul has no timeline.

You're unfolding

exactly as you need to.

Day 268

Make Space for Stillness

Even five quiet breaths

can remind you:

you are more than the rush.

Day 269

You're Allowed to Want Softness

A gentle life is not a lesser life.

It is a brave one.

Day 270

Let the Light Touch You

Even in your heaviness,

you are still worthy

of warmth and wonder.

Day 271

Pause Before You Push

Sometimes the urge to act

is a signal to rest.

Honor the pause.

Day 272

You Are Not Meant to Be Numb

Protecting yourself from pain

can also block joy.

Feel again.

Day 273

Let Life Surprise You with Ease

It doesn't always have to be hard.

Let something be easier than expected.

Day 274

You Can Shift Without Force

Change doesn't always require effort.

Sometimes it arrives

with grace.

Day 275

Let Love Be the Language

Speak it through your glance,

your silence,

your small, kind choices.

Day 276

You Don't Have to Chase Belonging

You belong by being.

You don't have to shape-shift

to be seen.

Day 277

Even the Ordinary Is Sacred

The stirring of a spoon,

the sound of birds—

all of it holy.

Day 278

Let Go of the "Someday" Life

Someday isn't promised.

Let beauty find you

in the now.

Day 279

You Are Allowed to Be Soft and Strong

You can be both.

You already are.

Day 280

This Moment Is a Threshold

Not just passing time—

a doorway.

Step through it awake.

Day 281

Trust Your Inner Timing

Your journey unfolds like the moon—

phases, pauses,

and quiet brilliance.

Day 282

You Can Be at Peace Without Having All the Pieces

Let peace come

even in the unfinished chapters.

Day 283

Honor What You've Survived

Your presence is proof.

You made it this far—

and that matters deeply.

Day 284

Let Your Breath Slow the Day

One deep inhale

can stretch time,

soften thought, invite peace.

Day 285

You Are Not Defined by Yesterday

You are allowed to outgrow

every story

you no longer fit.

Day 286

Let Kindness Begin Within

You don't need to be hard on yourself

to be motivated.

Let kindness move you forward.

Day 287

This Moment Is a Gift You Can Open

Even the quietest days

are wrapped in light

if you know where to look.

Day 288

You Can Walk Gently Through the World

Let your presence be

a balm,

a breath of ease.

Day 289

You Are Part of Something Vast

Beyond thoughts and plans,

you belong to the sky,

the rhythm, the stars.

Day 290

Let Silence Cleanse You

Step into the quiet

not to escape,

but to remember.

Day 291

You are whole.

even while you're growing

Becoming doesn't mean you're broken.

It means you are alive,

and changing with grace.

Day 292

Let the Day Unfold Without Judgment

It's okay if today isn't grand.

Let it be

what it is.

Day 293

Let Your Soul Take the Lead

When the mind spins,

place your hand on your heart—

and listen there.

Day 294

Feel the Wind, Trust the Change

Change may feel wild—

but it brings new air,

new direction, new light.

Day 295

Let Go of the Noise That Isn't Yours

You don't have to carry

everyone else's chaos.

Return to center.

Day 296

Breathe in Beauty, Breathe Out Worry

Let the breath

remind you

of what's real and near.

Day 297

You Are Allowed to Move Slowly

Speed does not equal value.

Let your steps be small,

intentional, true.

Day 304

Speak Gently to Your Becoming

You're still unfolding.

Speak to yourself

as you would to a blooming flower.

Day 305

Joy Is a Form of Wisdom

Trust the things

that make you smile

for no reason.

Day 306

Let Simplicity Hold You

Strip it all back—

to breath,

to sunlight, to truth.

Day 307

You're Allowed to Not Be Available

Say no.

Close the door.

Return to your own sacred space.

Day 308

Beauty Is Always Nearby

Even on the hardest days,

a bird sings.

A leaf glows. A breeze remembers you.

Day 309

Let Your Spirit Choose First

Not logic.

Not pressure.

Let your spirit vote with a yes or no.

Day 310

You Don't Have to Be Ready to Begin

The first step

can be shaky,

and still sacred.

Day 311

Be Present to the Quiet Miracles

Nothing explodes.

But everything shifts

when you pay attention.

Day 312

Let Rest Be Part of the Journey

Tired is not a flaw.

It's a message—

you deserve care.

Day 313

You Are Allowed to Protect Your Peace

Not all battles need your energy.

Choose silence,

choose stillness, choose peace.

Day 314

You Were Not Made to Hustle Through Life

You were made to breathe deeply,

to love freely,

to notice the sky.

Day 315

Listen for What Resonates

Not what's loudest—

but what feels like truth

deep in the bones.

Day 316

You Can Be Both Grateful and Growing

You can love where you are

and still dream forward.

It's not contradiction—it's an expansion.

Day 317

Let Life Be More Felt Than Figured Out

The mind wants answers.

The heart wants presence.

Choose the heart.

Day 318

Your Voice Carries Light

Speak what uplifts.

Speak what's real.

Your voice is part of the healing.

Day 319

Let This Breath Be Enough

No future fixing.

No past regretting.

Just this breath—alive, and enough.

Day 320

You Are Held by Something Vast

Call it grace, God, life, love—

but know:

you are never alone.

Day 321

Let Go of the Mask Today

You don't need to impress, pretend, or perform.

You're safe to be real.

That's where connection begins.

Day 322

Let the Quiet Guide You

Loud doesn't always mean true.

Follow the quiet thing inside

that feels like peace.

Day 323

You Can Choose Light Again

Even after darkness.

Even after doubt.

Light is always waiting.

Day 324

You're Not Behind—You're Becoming

There is no rush

to become who you already are

at your core.

Day 325

Let Your Yes Be Honest

Don't say yes

to please.

Say yes when your whole being agrees.

Day 326

You Are More Than Your Wounds

Your pain has shaped you,

but it does not define you.

You are vast.

Day 327

You Deserve a Life That Feels Good to Live

Not just manageable—

but beautiful,

authentic, and true.

Day 328

Let the Moment Hold You Open

Don't brace against life.

Let yourself soften

and be met.

Day 329

Even Small Shifts Matter

The tiniest change in direction

can transform

an entire journey.

Day 330

Release the Need to Be Certain

Certainty is a comfort,

but not a requirement.

Walk forward anyway.

Day 331

Let Today Be a Gentle Turning Point

No drama needed.

Just a breath,

and a shift in awareness.

Day 332

You Are Made of More Than Struggle

You are made of stars,

and softness,

and unexplainable resilience.

Day 333

Let What's Real Be What Remains

When the roles fall away,

what's left is truer

than anything you could pretend.

Day 334

There Is Power in Soft-Spoken Truth

You don't need to shout

to be heard by the soul.

Truth speaks for itself.

Day 335

You Don't Have to Prove Anything Today

Your worth is not on trial.

You woke up.

You are enough.

Day 336

Let the Natural World Recalibrate You

Stand barefoot.

Listen to the wind.

Let the Earth teach your nervous system peace.

Day 337

You Can Be Fully Here Without Knowing What's Next

Presence doesn't need a plan.

Just attention.

Just breath.

Day 338

Your Feelings Are Valid, Always

You don't need permission

to feel what you feel.

Let it rise. Let it pass.

Day 339

Let Kindness Be What You Leave Behind

A word, a glance, a moment.

Let your presence ripple

softness into the world.

Day 340

Let This Be the Day You Trust Again

In life.

In yourself.

In the unseen hand guiding it all.

Day 341

You Are Allowed to Change Your Mind

Growth often means outgrowing old truths.

You're free to evolve

into who you've become.

Day 342

Let Stillness Restore Your Spirit

Pause not to escape,

but to return

to yourself.

Day 343

You Don't Have to Earn Rest

Rest is not a reward.

It's a rhythm,

and you belong to it.

Day 344

Let Go of What Drains You

Protect your peace

like something sacred.

Because it is.

Day 345

You Are Worthy of a Gentle Life

One filled with presence,

not pressure.

One that feels like home.

Day 346

Let Softness Be a Way of Living

Soft words.

Soft footsteps.

Soft gaze. Live softly, and leave beauty.

Day 347

Even the Smallest Light Illuminates

Don't underestimate your impact.

Even a candle

can warm the dark.

Day 348

You Are Not What Happened to You

You are what you've become

despite it.

You are healing in motion.

Day 349

Let Peace Be a Daily Practice

Not something to wait for—

but something you choose

again and again.

Day 350

You Are the Answer You've Been Seeking

Come home to yourself.

You are the love,

the light, the clarity.

Day 351

Let Your Truth Be a Quiet Flame

It doesn't need to burn loud—

just steady,

and real.

Day 352

You Can Love Without Fear

Love doesn't require perfection.

It asks only presence,

and the courage to open.

Day 353

Let Simplicity Set You Free

Less doing.

More being.

Let life be uncluttered and rich.

Day 354

You Don't Need to Wait to Feel Alive

Aliveness is not in the future.

It's here,

in the breath you're breathing now.

Day 355

Let Grace Be Your Default

For yourself.

For others.

Let compassion speak first.

Day 356

The Ordinary Is Full of Light

Nothing is too small

to be holy

when seen with clear eyes.

Day 357

You Are Safe to Trust Your Joy

Joy is not a trick.

It's truth,

in its most radiant form.

Day 358

Let Every Ending Hold a Seed

Nothing truly ends.

Everything becomes

something else.

Day 359

Your Soul Is Unshaken

Life may tremble,

but your essence

remains steady.

Day 360

Live From the Inside Out

Let your inner truth

shape your outer steps.

That's how authenticity breathes.

Day 361

You Are the Calm You Crave

Peace isn't out there.

It's in how you meet

what's here.

Day 362

Let This Moment Teach You

Truth reveals itself

in stillness, in breath,

in your own direct experience.

Day 363

You Are a Reminder of What's Possible

Your healing,

your honesty,

your light—it inspires.

Day 364

Let Today Be Light-Filled

Not perfect.

Not easy.

Just light-filled, in even one small way.

Day 365

You Are a Living Miracle

The fact that you breathe,

that you feel,

that you love—this is sacred.

Please give yourself

the permission you need today

to return home—
home to your

Authentic state of Being:

Loving Awareness.

The world may have pulled you in many directions.
You may have worn masks, played roles, or carried
the weight of expectations.

But beneath it all, you remain who you truly are:
a living expression of peace, presence, and love.

Let today be the day you soften, breathe, and
remember.
You don't need to earn it.
You don't need to chase it.
You are it.

Come home to *Loving Awareness.*
Let it be enough.
Let it be your Strength.

Dedication

I dedicate this book to the children,
and to the children's children—

That they may know true Joy,
that they may live in Peace & Happiness,
and that they may help heal the ills of our world.

Thank you. Thank you. Thank you.
I love you. I love you. I love you.